I0483909

FIRE UP YOUR SALES FIGURES

How To Win More Customers And Influence Them To Buy From You

"Profit in business comes from repeat customers, customers that boast about your project or service, and that bring friends with them'

W. Edwards Deming

Special Dedication

To every salesperson in the world. More specifically, this book is
for that salesperson who is committed towards making a
difference in the world.

Disclaimer

ISBN: -10: 1507758782   **ISBN-13:** 978-1507758786

Contents

If It Must Happen Then It's Up To You

'The quality of a person's life is in direct proportion to their commitment to excellence, regardless of their chosen field of endeavor'

Vince Lombard

In life, we seldom get a second chance to make that very vital first impression. When meeting a client for the very first time; be it over the phone, or physically, remember that you are the first product. And no, you are not going to replace the product and market yourself as the product. Being the first product as a salesperson is to understand that most people buy based on what they *see*. The killer here lies in adequate preparation and good grooming. Know what to say, when to say it, and how to say it.

Avoid imitating other people. You will end up being either a faint copy or a lower version of them. However much you try, you can never be somebody else. Be the best version of yourself. You have unlimited capabilities to tap into, once you learn to use your power of self belief, and to never be afraid of exercising what you believe in. Be yourself. There is a uniqueness and originality that you represent in this world. This is where your true self-worth and potential lies.

As a salesperson, you are always an option towards accessing the product by the customer. Even in your absence, the customer can still have access to the same product. Therefore, your first target role is to lure the customer to trust and use you as the only suitable link to the product. Yes, the customer may have many options towards the product, but your option should appear as the sole best.

Be neat and smell fresh. Prepare well. This is what should differentiate you from the rest of the competition. You should have lots of FAQ's about the product and the relevant answers. Know what to tell the customer, when to say it, and how to say it.

Motivate yourself

You are the master of your own ship, with all the navigation passwords at your disposal. As much as you cannot control what goes on in your environment, you have the authority over the choices of your reaction to your circumstances. Sometimes, the sales process can turn out to be a very daunting task, even though it doesn't have to be. You must constantly find ways of motivating yourself. This will give you the tenacity and drive to succeed.

One of the greatest world boxing heroes; Mohamed Ali, was once asked how many sit-ups he was doing in his daily practices. And his response was, 'I don't count my sit-ups when I start, I only start counting when I begin to feel the pain associated with doing the sit-ups; because that's when real counting matters.'

Set personal goals and be committed towards achieving them. This will always provoke you to go an extra mile in your efforts in order to succeed. At the end of the day, you work for yourself. Any results out of your work will be directly reflected in your life. You are never doing it just for the clients alone; you will always be the biggest beneficiary of your efforts. Always motivate yourself knowing that if it must happen, then it is always up to you.

What Really Counts At The End Of The Day Is Making A Sale

I've always found that anything worth achieving will always have obstacles in the way and you've got to have that drive and determination to overcome those obstacles on route to whatever it is that you want to accomplish'

Chuck Norris

At the end of the day, it won't matter how pleasing you were before the eyes of the customer. It won't matter how well dressed you were on that day. It won't matter whether you visited the client on foot, or by a luxurious car. What really counts at the close of that day is whether you were able to make a sale (or in some instances, a positive commitment from the client towards a buying the product at a later date). Period!

Today's purchasing trends suggests that people tend to buy more of the things they want rather than the things they need. This kills the perception of strictly focusing the product's sale to the needs of the customers.

Some clients will want to promise you that they would wish to make purchases to your products in the future, and not at the moment when you are selling to them. Get such clients to commit to buying the products, either by giving you some 'deposits', or they should give you definite dates upon which you should contact them in the future. Be wary of clients who may want to promise you about buying any of your products, just to get rid of your presence.

When meeting any sort of client, high class or low class, accord the necessary attention. There are moments when you might wrongly misjudge a client to be having the potential to easily buy any of your products, only to be discouraged by their inability. On the contrary, there are too, other times when you might wrongly misjudge a client's inability to buy any of your products, only to be proved otherwise by those clients.

Be greedy for more sales leads. Over the years as a successful sales executive, I always learnt to at least meet three new clients on each passing day, and an equal number of clients from my referral lists. It worked wonders in return.

To be successful in sales, you must have a plan and spread wide your net in order to bag in more and more customers; day in day out. Ask for leads from your friends, colleagues, superiors, current and previous clients. Ask for leads even when you contact new prospects. There more the leads you have, the higher chances you will have in converting some of those leads into successful sales. What really counts at the end of the day is making a sale

Put On Your Sales Armor, Confidence

'Believe in yourself! Have faith in your abilities! Without a humble but reasonable confidence in your own powers you cannot be successful or happy'

Norman Vincent Peale

Perhaps you have heard that most customers buy 'confidence'. However, nobody is born with self confidence, and neither is self confidence an inheritable gene. But you absolutely need to be confident enough in order to be able to convincingly, advise any client to take up any of your products. You too need to have confidence in order to effectively sustain any sales conversation or negotiation with a client.

Self confidence is a virtue earned from repeated practice; year in year out, until it becomes part and parcel of your system. A number of persons who begin their careers in sales often feel nervous when facing groups or clients for the very first time. Sometimes it is ok to feel that way, though it is not always comfortable. Self confidence and sales go hand in hand. Learn to face your fears and confront them. Always remember that fear is simply some scary picture you have created and housed in your mind. That scary picture only exists in your mind, it is nowhere in reality.

Bill Gates; the founder of Microsoft, was once quoted as saying that, 'The world doesn't care about your self esteem. The world will expect you to do something before you feel good about something.' With self confidence, you will literally 'move mountains' in your sales career. You will seek to sell to the 'elephant customers' and in return bring value to your organization and to yourself.

Fear may want to hold you back. It will try to show you bigger and bigger mountains that actually never exist in any reality. It will want to drag you to the path of normalcy; where you will never be able to stretch your limits. Will Smith; the famous Hollywood Actor, is a perfect example on how to attack fears.

During an interview with one of the American Televisions, he confessed that he hated being scared to do something. That it was that fear of fear itself which motivated him to attack his fears.

In the bible, there are references of great men and women whom God used to perform great miracles of the time, even though they had fear in their own lives. The story of Moses and the Israelites is a perfect example. At first, Moses never believed in himself and in the role which God offered him. Nonetheless, with all of his doubts, God walked with him and guided him as he successfully led the Israelites away from the land of Pharaoh. You have to take small leaps of faith while confronting your fears on a daily basis.

The same Bible reminds us about one of the teachings of Jesus. He said that if we ask, seek and knock then, we will be given, we shall find and the door will be opened for us, respectively. Do not allow anything to intimidate you. You are the perfect image of God the almighty. If you believe in something then go out and get it. We are temporarily here on earth. So be the best that you can be; to yourself and to the society. Rise above your fears and conquer the world.

Don't Open Your Mouth If You Can't Listen

'One of the most sincere forms of respect is actually listening to what another has to say'

Bryant H. McGill

You are only a link to the product. As a salesperson, you should know that you are just but one link between the customer and the product. Even without you, there are still other links between the client and the product. The client can still have access to the product, through other ways i.e. through fellow salespeople. Therefore, if you fail to effectively listen to your clients, then it won't take long before they find another salesperson who will listen to them; and you can foretell the end result.

You must learn to effectively listen to your prospects/clients during sales conversations. They way you would perceive any issue related to a product may be totally different from the way some of your clients would perceive the same issue. It may be true that you need to take charge of a sales conversation, but that doesn't necessarily mean that you should unnecessarily dominate the talk without ceasing. When you talk over and over without giving the client an opportunity to respond to you, it would be equivalent to talking to a wall. In fact, the most precise likening would be talking to yourself and expecting the client to buy into your self-talk.

During sales conversations, you must demonstrate to the clients that you are genuinely interested and concerned about any issues that they may want to raise. The best approach you can use is the rule of the thumb; 'listen to them in the same way and manner that you would want them to listen to you'. And when you do so, you will have a perfect chance to determine the selling points of your products to them.

Listening to clients will hand you an invaluable opportunity to ask them the right questions; some of which would most probably lead you into closing sales. But most significant, if you effectively listen to your clients, you will be able to establish their real needs.

Also, you will get to know any of their fears, and subsequently secure any other relevant feedback which might help you in future product's improvement.

Be Masculine But Act Feminine

'I choose gentleness... Nothing is won by force. I choose to be gentle. If I raise my voice may it be only in praise. If I clench my fist, may it be only in prayer. If I make a demand, may it be only of myself'

Max Lucado

This approach is best applied during the processes of prospecting or during negotiations. Be strong in you resolve to succeed no matter what obstacles falling on your way. The obstacles may be in form of: customers switching off their phones during conversations, customers bluntly resisting your products, having inadequate resources to effectively assist you reach clients, hectic and unending traffic jams on your way to seeing clients, uncomfortable weather, gossip and ridicule from fellow employees, etc. You must be strong willed (masculine), in order to overcome any challenge which may face you on each passing day.

But be feminine in your actual selling approach. This does not mean you putting on make ups and dressing like a lady in case you are a man. No! It means that you have to be gentle and enthusiastic while meeting or while engaging with your prospects. If you have a meeting, be the first person to arrive at the venue of the meeting. If the meeting is at the prospects' place of work, then ensure that you arrive on time. Let the customers know that you are deeply interested in their needs.

When a client gives you an opportunity for a meeting, aim to always leave such a meeting having given the client a personal touch. Out of a million salespeople out there in the market, leave the customer with the feeling that he/she can only access the product through you.

A successful sales process is like a sweet seduction process which eventually flourishes into marriage. Do not let any stone untouched during your sales conversations with clients: relate all the customer's needs with the product's benefits, and the best ending should be the product being in possession of the client.

Products and services are designed for consumers; customers. Salespersons should therefore act as mere conduits of accessing the products by the clients, or in some cases, temporary custodians of the products on behalf of the customers. Do not keep in your possession for too long what is not fully meant for you. If you effectively practice this then it will translate into more sales and subsequently, a fat paycheck.

Be Different, And Release Your Inner Child

'I will prepare and some day my chance will come'

Abraham Lincoln

Almost anyone can sell. As long as you can engage anyone in any form conversation, then you probably can sell. That's why today, there are more salespeople across the globe as compared to any other profession. But against this multitude of salespersons, there are only a bunch of successful salespersons.

Successful salespeople are unique and creative. They literally 'eat and dream' about creative ways of approaching and selling in the growing number of new market segments. To join this list of successful salespeople, you must too be different. If you have been calling ten clients in a day, then it's time to upgrade and call thirty of them in a day. If you have been coming late to the office on each morning, then it's time to change and be the first person to arrive. If you have been meeting only one or two clients in a day, then it's time to adjust and start meeting at least five of them in aday. If you have never cold-called any client, then it's time to cold-call ten of them in a day, and thereafter upgrade the number. To expect different results, you must adopt a different approach.

Be different. If you must change the people around you in order to improve on your figures then don't hesitate to do so. Spend more time with the top performers in your organization, and get to know what they could be doing right that you aren't. Don't be afraid at trying out any new idea which you believe can have a positive impact on your sales. Remember that you will always miss 100% of the chances you do not take. Boldly, try out those new ideas, and in the event that you fail, then you will have had a perfect opportunity to learn from your mistakes, and thereafter make necessary amends for your success in future.

Readily, seek out for that which you can easily give back, not for what you would cling on to. If everyone was to cling on whatever they cherish, then life would lose its meaning.

I recently watched Pastor Joel over the television, as he delivered one of his sermons. Specifically, during that memorable sermon, he brought my attention to one of the burdens that many of us unnecessarily carry along as we go about day to day living. He narrated a story of a man who had grown of age and decided to take a closer look at the way he had lived over the years. And that this man arrived at these conclusions: *'That when I was a child, up to the time when I reached 18, what goes around me never bothered me. Between eighteen to forty five (18-45) years, I took so much interest on what was going on in my life and my environment. I suspected so much, and could even hear even imaginary sounds of people talking and gossiping about me. Between my retirement age, up to now that I am seventy nine (79) years, my inner feelings have recycled back to when I was a child. I have even realized that nobody cares about what I do or even what I think. It is all my responsibility. If only I knew this during my active working years...............'*

Be enthusiastic, open minded, approachable, and then simply go out there in pursuit of making a sale. You are in charge of your life and your destiny. And there is never any way out! You simply must make it or make it; this is the right spirit and attitude you need to put on each passing day. Sell with the spirit of a small child; knowing that that is what counts at the end of the day. Release your inner child in your selling.

Loosen Up

'Let yourself be open and life will be easier. A spoon of salt in a glass of water makes the water undrinkable. A spoon of salt in a lake is almost unnoticed'

Buddha Siddhartha Guatama Shakyamuni

Have you ever told someone something funny but waited in vain for the person to laugh or even smile? That is the feeling you receive when you engage with people who have not loosen up. During sales conversations with clients, be the way you would want your customers to be. You can't frown in front of them and expect them to be the opposite.

When meeting clients, be genuinely enthusiastic and happy. Being happy will radiate into your customers, and the end result will be a fulfilling conversation. Do not fake your happiness, simply let it flow. I guess that you are aware that happiness in one of the virtues which is hard to fake.. If you are not happy then you are simply not happy. No matter how hard you try to fake it, it will eventually come out.

You may have been trapped in the unmoving traffic for long hours on your way to see a client, or walked on foot under dire weather conditions to meet a client, etc. Desist from exposing your socio-economic struggles to the customer. They may want to avoid you, so as to keep you away from such struggles. Instead, you've got to be grateful and happy. You may have undergone through certain struggles but ended up closing a sale, while your colleague elsewhere may have had it smooth, but missed on making any sale

There is an anonymous statement which I have cherished over the years. In fact, I have used it on a number of my books to encourage anyone who may be faced with an adversity. It's titled, *Always look around*. Sometimes selling can turn out to be a draining undertaking. Disappointments, discouragements and hopelessness may sometimes engulf even the strongest of salespeople. In such moments, you should *look around*. Below is the excerpt of *Always look around*.

Always Look Around

I once lacked what to eat, and then I met a man who had no teeth!

I once lacked good shoes to wear, and then I met a man who had no feet!

I once had no shirt to wear, and then I met a man who had no arms!

I once lacked money, and then I met a dead beggar on a street!

Anonymous

When your life is on the downhill and you seem to be totally defeated, don't ever give up. Out there, someone else has it even worse. When you look around, you'll be glad that your world isn't that worse. Your life could only seem to be an endless curse if you choose to lock yourself in your own world, and refuse to look around.

Always Look Around

Remember The Proverbial Story Of Rome

'Rome wasn't built in a day'

Age-Old Adage

Remember the age-old adage, 'Rome wasn't built in a day.' Effective and successful selling is like a game of Chess: it takes time and pretty well calculated moves. It is like that sweet wine which may need enough time to effectively ferment.

Selling is not an instant money making undertaking. No. The main focus of an effective salesperson should be to correctly match the needs of a customer with the benefits of the product at hand.

Do not just merely push clients into buying products. There are those clients who would wish to seek the opinion of their colleagues, spouses, or friends (read about the four types of clients you must meet in every market). Respect the wishes of such clients; but ensure you alert them about your intention to follow up on them in future.

An effective sales process should be a fulfilling undertaking which should successfully lead clients to purchasing the offered products. After closing any sale, the customer and the salesperson should be like anew united family ready to start a new journey together. This can never be realized when you hastily sell products to clients; they may even fail to remember you.

Do Not Focus On Making A Sale Just For Survival Ends

'Real integrity is doing the right thing, knowing that nobody's going to know whether you did it or not'

Oprah Winfrey

Trying to sell a product just for survival ends is the most desperate approach to any sales. That your focus is simply to sell that product in order to meet certain urgent/emergent needs from your side. This is what I would refer to as embarking on a desperate mission. It is brought about by lack of personal drive, and short focus in the sales career. It is provoked by warning letters from employers; advising salespersons of the intended termination of their contracts or services should the employer fail to note certain positive improvements in their sales.

During my sales career, one of my best friends was issued with a warning letter: that unless he met a specific sales target, his sales contract was going to be liable for termination. Honestly, he thought that the world was coming to its end. He felt physically threatened, and outwardly looked frightened. However, this was not the original intention of the employer. The employer simply wanted a justification as to why my friend deserved a continuation in salary payments.

I had on certain occasions accompanied this friend to meet some his clients and believe you me; He really struggled to make it happen. Deep inside his heart, I could smell that he yearned to make quick sales, but a number of his customers took their sweet time before picking up the products.

And I learnt one very vital lesson in sales, *never to wait until everything turns into an emergency*. No matter what, you should never appear to be desperate before any client. They may avoid you or rather give you 'convincing' reasons as to why the product does not fit their needs.

You understand yourself better. The best time to be desperate is during your research/preparations for sales. When you are alone and planning on which clients to contact and how best to sell to them. Be desperate while researching on things which would lead you to closing a deal with any client.

Understand Your Organization

If you know where you are coming from, it's easy to figure where you are headed to

Anonymous

How much do you know about your organization? One of the biggest mistakes made by a number of salespersons is in having incomplete understanding about their organizations. In the eyes of the customer, you are your organization. Know the structure of your company; from down the pyramid to the top. It would be uncomfortable to be updated by the customers about events happening in your organization. Be on top of things.

As a salesperson, you are the number one trustee of your organization's image before the eyes of the public. This is because you are the direct link between the customer and the organization; through the product. You must yearn to safeguard this enormous responsibility bestowed upon you.

Almost all companies, organizations or institutions have general guidelines of conducting their businesses. They have certain core values, missions, and objectives to achieve within certain specific set times. You must be at the forefront in spreading all the core values of your organization to the clients. Be passionate about the core values that your organization holds in high esteem.

Understanding you organization demands that you know all about the latest changes in the management of the organization, all the organization's products, anticipated new products, a number of your fellow employees, a number of your top rated clients etc. You should never murmur in response to a client's inquiry about your company.

The Most Effective Way To Close A Sales Presentation

'Nothing in this world can take the place of persistence. Talent will not: nothing is more common than unsuccessful men with talent. Genius will not; unrewarded genius is almost a proverb. Education will not: the world is full of educated derelicts. Persistence and determination alone are omnipotent'

Calvin Coolidge

The most effective way to close any sales presentation is not in making any actual sales, but is in walking away from that presentation with a feeling that you have honestly made the customer fully aware of the product's benefits. And when a client makes any purchase based on such a presentation, then be rest assured that that client would be yours to lose.

What most salespeople forget is that clients are just fellow human beings. They too have feelings and reasons as to why they should purchase or not purchase certain products or services. Treat your clients with honesty and integrity.

Nobody wants to be lied to, not even you. Therefore, handle your clients in the same manner and way that you would wish to be handled if the client was the salesperson and you were now client. You need those same clients in the future, but weirdly, those same clients might not necessarily need your services or products in the future.

Make The Product The King

We all matter — maybe less than a lot
but always more than none

John Green

There is a common connotation doing endless rounds in customer service that the customer is always the King. Equally, there is another suggestion in credit management, that money is the King. In selling, the product therefore should be the King. Yes the customer may always be right, and will always continue to play the big brother's role, however, for you to effectively sell any product, you must have the undying belief that the customer can never survive without purchasing that product.

To most salespeople; especially the ones dealing in solution selling, or selling new products, it is imperative to have a belief in the product or service you are offering, before going out to meet with clients. More specifically, the role of any salesperson in a start-up business is therefore well cut out; to awaken the minds of targeted consumers, and convince them out of their *normalcy* (out of the products or services that they are perhaps used to). And the only way to achieve this is by believing that the product has the best solution to the client's needs, as compared to any other product that the customer may be used to.

A good number of products and services are perfectly designed with the targeted customers at their center of focus. What remains for the salesperson is simply to link the correct customers with the correct products; using cost effective means.

The only way the product will be able to dislodge the customer at the throne, is by the product being 'a must have' necessity to the customers. Make the product the king by believing in it before going out to sell it. Truth be told, you have no role in trying to sell any product or service that you have doubts in its value to the targeted clients.

Never Forget Your Footsteps

'Yes, I'm a great optimist. But, when trying to make a decision, I often think of the worst case scenario. I call it 'the eaten by wolves factor.' If I do something, what's the most terrible thing that could happen? Would I be eaten by wolves? One thing that makes it possible to be an optimist is if you have a contingency plan for when all hell breaks loose. There are a lot of things I don't worry about, because I have a plan in place if they do'

Randy Pausch, The Last Lecture

In the events that you either succeed or fail in closing any sale, don't forget to have the client's contact details. Equally, give the client your contact details.

As you close your talks, remind the customer of your intention to contact him/her in the future: to seek for his/her feedback on the product, to ask for more leads/referrals, or to proceed with the conversation, in case of any previous 'deadlock' in your sales conversations.

You should immediately diarize any agreed or suggested follow up dates. If you do this in the presence of clients, then they will have a feeling that you are surely committed to sorting out their needs.

The Four Types Of Clients You Must Meet In Every Market

'By failing to prepare, you are preparing to fail'

Benjamin Franklin

- **The Empathizers**

The Empathizers are every salesperson's dream clients. Most probably, the empathizers have a feel of what it means to try to sell any product to any client, and would therefore, readily embrace and encourage any salesperson they come across.

The empathizers have no problem in allocating part of their time in order to gain more understanding on what any salesperson has to offer. Generally, the empathizers are usually warm, welcoming, and most significant, understanding.

- **The Analyzers**

Just like the empathizers, the analyzers equally have no problem in spending some time with any salesperson; towards understanding the products on offer. However, the analyzers are the 'take me slowly' type of clients.

They do not want to be rushed through any sales process, and do have question after question when meeting with salespeople. Naturally, the analyzers aren't 'slow' but just do not want to miss anything about the product.

While anticipating a sales meeting with the analyzer a salesperson should have all the relevant information about the product or service. Equally, they should try to gather as much information as they can about the competition, and creatively align their sales pitch to please the analyzers.

- **The Inquisitive Clients**

  They are very sensitive and extremely curious. They always want more and more details on the products or services.

  Significantly, they usually make their purchases after deep analysis, and further consultation of people they trust; like close friends, relatives, spouses, neighbors etc.

  They may be a nightmare to sell to, however, if you are successful at selling to them, then they are the type of clients who you can keep for life.

- **The wild at hearts**

  Mostly during cold calls, they are the type of clients who will first wonder a lot where you have obtained their contacts.

  In some extreme cases, they are the clients who will want to prohibit you from trying to contact them in future.

  They are often moody and unpredictable. They are usually quick to tell you 'yes', while in reality, they mean the opposite which is 'no'. Selling successfully to the wild at hearts is often a game of probability.

Why Customers May Not Want To Buy From You

Write it on your heart that every day is the best day in the year. He is rich who owns the day, and no one owns the day who allows it to be invaded with fret and anxiety. Finish every day and be done with it. You have done what you could. Some blunders and absurdities, no doubt crept in. Forget them as soon as you can, tomorrow is a new day; begin it well and serenely, with too high a spirit to be cumbered with your old nonsense. This new day is too dear, with its hopes and invitations, to waste a moment on the yesterdays'

Ralph Waldo Emerson,

It can really be disheartening to devote all your energies towards selling certain products / services in the market, only to be met by unending customer objections and rejections. You may have rightly targeted the most ideal markets for your products with the right marketing messages and sales approaches, but still end up with paltry responses from the targeted clients. It is therefore very essential to understand some of the top six reasons as to why potential clients would object to buying any of your products or services.

Below are the top six reasons why clients may object to buying any of your products or services.

- **Negative recommendations from past, unsatisfied clients**

  A good product or service recommendation from satisfied clients may bring in more sales and sales leads as compared to a paid up advertisement in any local media. And on the contrary, negative recommendations from unsatisfied clients may drive away more sales and sales leads.

  This therefore, means that you must effectively handle negative customer feedbacks. One of the best ways of sorting out such negative feedbacks is by first establishing the real facts/issues behind any client's dissatisfaction. A customer may get dissatisfied out of a poor service, purchasing of faulty products, or by purchasing products/services at exorbitant prices which are not commensurate with the value of the goods/services offered.

In order to effectively contain such negative complaints: you should find ways of apologizing to the affected clients and promise them of a better experience next time; in case of a previous poor service. You can equally offer to replace a faulty/damaged product, or offer a reasonably good discount on their next purchase(s).

Dissatisfied clients are like poison to any business. They can resort to 'poisoning' other potential clients and this in return, can literally bring any business to its knee, if not effectively handled.

- **They have a need, but your product/service doesn't match that need**

  Why would you want to sell charcoal to a family who have just ran out of gas, and have requested that you help them re-fill their gas cylinder? First, get them the gas cylinder filled up, and thereafter you can consider tempting them to settle for a secondary source of energy.

  There are growing numbers of persons who have soft spots for certain specific brands of products/services. If it's a car, you will always find them specifically with a Mercedes Benz, or specifically with a BMW, and etc. You will never catch them inside any other car brand.

  They do not like to mix up their taste for brands. They value their taste, and would not trade anything for it. If it's a soda, you may find them religiously adhering to drinking either cola flavored, orange flavored, gingered flavored, etc drinks. If it's alcoholic drinks, then they will strictly be drinking beer and not other hard drink(s); they will be drinking one specific brand of beer.

When the features or benefits of your product matches the needs of clients, then no matter how long it takes, you will be able to make a sale, in the fullness of time.

- **Lack of information about the product**

    Take yourself in the shoes of any client and ask yourself, if you would make any purchase to a product that you have no information on where to find it, how to use it, or what you can use it for? That would be a definite and a resounding no. It is like expecting the clients to make purchases to products that do not exist. (Naturally, when you do not know about any product, then it doesn't exist in your world).

    Before you hurriedly, expect clients to hand over to you their hard earned money in exchange for any product, ensure that they have enough information on the product. Possibly, they should be able to tell what the product is all about: its purpose, its value, how to use it, etc.

    If it's a new product, then you should engage in lots of forums which should allow you to create necessary product awareness. Equally, take time to listen to client's questions, or their specific needs out of the products, so that you can have an opportunity to match the product's benefits with the specific needs of the clients.

- **Bad product experience**

    One stain that is always indelible in the minds of most clients is a poor product experience. That you heap lots of praise on say a blender, only for the gadget to blow up or fail to function once bought by a client! It would be difficult for any client to forget such an experience.

Most salespeople usually heap lots of unnecessary praises on the features and benefits of certain products, only for such products to yield contrary results once purchased by clients. A poor product experience is worse off than not making any sale at all. It may create a monster in the name of a bitter and vengeful customer. And who knows the boundaries of such bitter or vengeful clients?

In order to be at the safe zone, a salesperson should always ensure that all products availed for sale in any given market, matches their advertised/hyped values, qualities, and benefits. Always check on the functionality plus expiry date of any given product before you hand it over to the client. You would rather not sell any product for a given period of time, than to rush into selling a substandard product.

- **Poor handling**

Customers too are human. It is a dominant longing for everyone to be accorded a handling experience which is commensurate with their social status in the society. That's why titles like very important persons (VIPs) do exist in our midst.

Poor customer handling usually happens when: a salesperson takes too long before attending to a client, rushing a client over an inquiry or a sales process, failing to patiently and properly listen to customers' questions, communication breakdown, etc. Shockingly, there are growing record number of cases of ugly confrontations between salespeople and clients, in relation to poor customer handling?

The most effective way to handle clients is by using the age old 'Do unto others what you would wish to be done unto.' Salespersons should offer their clients, a service which is commensurate with what they could have wished for to be offered, if they were to play the role of a customer.

- **They simply lack purchasing power**

    After all that beautiful sales presentation, it is every salespersons' wish that a client would definitely purchase a given product or service. However, without the necessary client's purchasing ability, then making that sale would just be just but an elusive dream.

    You can't fight with clients who have no purchasing power for them to buy any of your products. Customers may lack purchasing ability due to several factors: unemployment, loss of job, financial constrains, lack of source of income, etc.

    However right your marketing message might be appealing, or however low your product's price may be, if a client lacks purchasing ability, especially at the time when you expect them to buy any of your products, then he/she will not.

    The best way to handle clients with no or less purchasing ability is to give them time. If they really have a need for the product or service, then they will definitely, do everything within their reach, in order to consolidate the necessary resources towards securing the item on offer.

Equally, they may just be lacking enough cash to purchase the actual product on offer. However, they might be having a potential to purchase the same product but in other tastes or versions. i.e. You might be selling a whole dozen of bar soap yet they have a potential of purchasing just one bar of that soap.

Be patient with such clients and never ignore them, because sooner or later, they may turn out to be your top rated clients.

Reasons Why Consumers Buy What They Buy

'The aim of marketing is to know and understand the customer so well the product or service fits him and sells itself'

Peter Drucker.

The ultimate goal of any produced product is for it to reach its intended market, and finally to its consumers. The real task for any salesperson is therefore, to identify where these customers could be located and avail to them these products.

It is proverbial that one man's meat is another man's poison. What may interest me out of any product, may not necessarily interest the next person. Across the globe, we all have divergent tastes and preferences for certain goods or services. It is therefore, very important to understand some of the common reasons as to why consumers would buy certain products.

Below are the top six reasons why any consumers buy what they buy.

- **They have a need, and there exists a product or service in the market that meets that need**

  This is the top most reason as to why people buy what they buy. If the car has ran out of gas, you would be headed to the gas station to have it re-filled. If you have a toothache, you would be headed to your dentist to have your tooth checked. Anyone who wants to purchase a nice cloth would be headed to a store retailing such clothes; it would be very difficult to find someone looking for a cloth in a food restaurant, not unless the food restaurant has a segment dealing with clothes.

  Consumers may not necessarily care about specific people selling certain products or services. What they are deeply interested in or concerned with, are the specific products that they are after. They more often go after products or services that meet their specific needs, save for countable cases of impulse buying.

- **They are in pursuit of value for their money**

  A growing number of people today are cautious on their spending. On top of most shopping lists today, there is a demand for value for money utilized. However pricey a product may seem, if its value matches its price, then such a product would be consumers' favorite.

  You are always that first client to your products. If you were to purchase that product at that given price, would you have secured value for your money? This is one question that you must ask yourself before going out to sell any product or service. Should you establish that a product you are offering for sale would not offer you value for its price, then that's the same feedback that such a product would receive from its intended clients. If you however choose to just go ahead and sell it, then be rest assured of registering more dissatisfied cases.

- **Good recommendations from previous satisfied clients**

  A good product recommendation from a satisfied consumer may bring in more sales and sales leads as compared to a paid up advertisement in any given local media. That's how powerful customer reviews and recommendations are. Such positive recommendations usually end up making undecided clients to eventually make up their minds and make purchases of the products under focus. Interestingly, in some instances, such feedbacks may push some consumers to make purchases for products and or services that they honestly do not need; to the advantage of the salesperson.

- **Convenient products**

An anonymous best put it, *that we currently live in a microwave society*. And truth be told, most people across the globe are in need of products that are easy and more convenient to use, and would readily embrace and purchase such products. A typical example in the poultry segment is the availability of already prepared chicken meat, ready for consumption, in most supermarket shelves. Most people are never interested in the deep rooted processes of products that they purchase; they are simply on the look for the ready-to-use kind of products.

Equally, customers would readily buy goods and services which are conveniently made available at the hour of their need. They detest undergoing any form of strain, before reaching to products of their desires. Convenient products help clients to save on time, and possibly, on money.

- **Freebies**

Who doesn't love free gifts? I guess that we almost all do love freebies, especially if given out in good faith. However, most consumers aren't necessarily looking out for free goods or free services, but are in pursuit of those products or services that might help them save on a few coins.

Clients love seasonal, or occasional discounts on purchases, or free samples (in case of new products) Consumers will find it hard to ever forget such kind gestures and you may be surprised to pull a good number of them from your competition if you accord them such freebies.

- **Credible and reliable products**

  Almost all consumers are looking out for credible and reliable products. In a world filled with counterfeit products, consumers usually embrace new products with lots of reservations. They want some assurance that the products they are purchasing are reliable enough to live their advertised purposes. Occasionally, they make a few purchases in order to allow them go and try out such new products, and will always re-surface to make future purchases, should such products meet or exceed their expectations.